Catching the Sun

Contents

Saynday and the Sun   **2**
Maui and the Sun   **12**

Folk tales and legends have been told for many years. They tell stories about people, places, or animals. Many folk tales or legends are the same even though they are from different countries.

Retold by Michele Paul
Illustrated by Ireen Denton

Sayuday and the Sun

A Native American Folk Tale

Saynday was a hero of the
Kiowa Indians.

Long ago, the sun only shone on one side of the world. The other side was always dark.

One day Saynday was out walking on the dark side of the world when he met Fox, Deer, and Magpie.

"You look so sad," said Saynday. "What's the matter with you?"

"It's this side of the world," said the animals. "It's too dark."

"We'll have to do something about it then," said Saynday.

So Saynday and the animals sat thinking. Soon Saynday had a plan.

"We could get the sun from the other side of the world," he said. "But we need someone to run far and fast."

Fox said, "I can run fast for a long way."

Deer said, "I can run fast, too, but I cannot run as far as Fox."

And Magpie said, "I can only run a very short way."

Then, Saynday told the animals his plan. Fox was to go to the side of the world where the sun lived. It was a long way, and it would take Fox a very long time to get there. Saynday said that Fox had to make friends with the Sun People. Fox had to stay with the Sun People until they trusted him.

So Fox set off to the light side of the world. When he got there he watched the Sun People. They had long spears and were playing a game with the sun. They were hitting the sun like a ball. Fox stayed with the Sun People for a long time. They showed him how to play their game and hold the sun.

One day, when they were all playing the game, Fox knew it was the right time. Fox got the sun and began to run. He ran as fast as he could. The Sun People didn't know what Fox was doing.

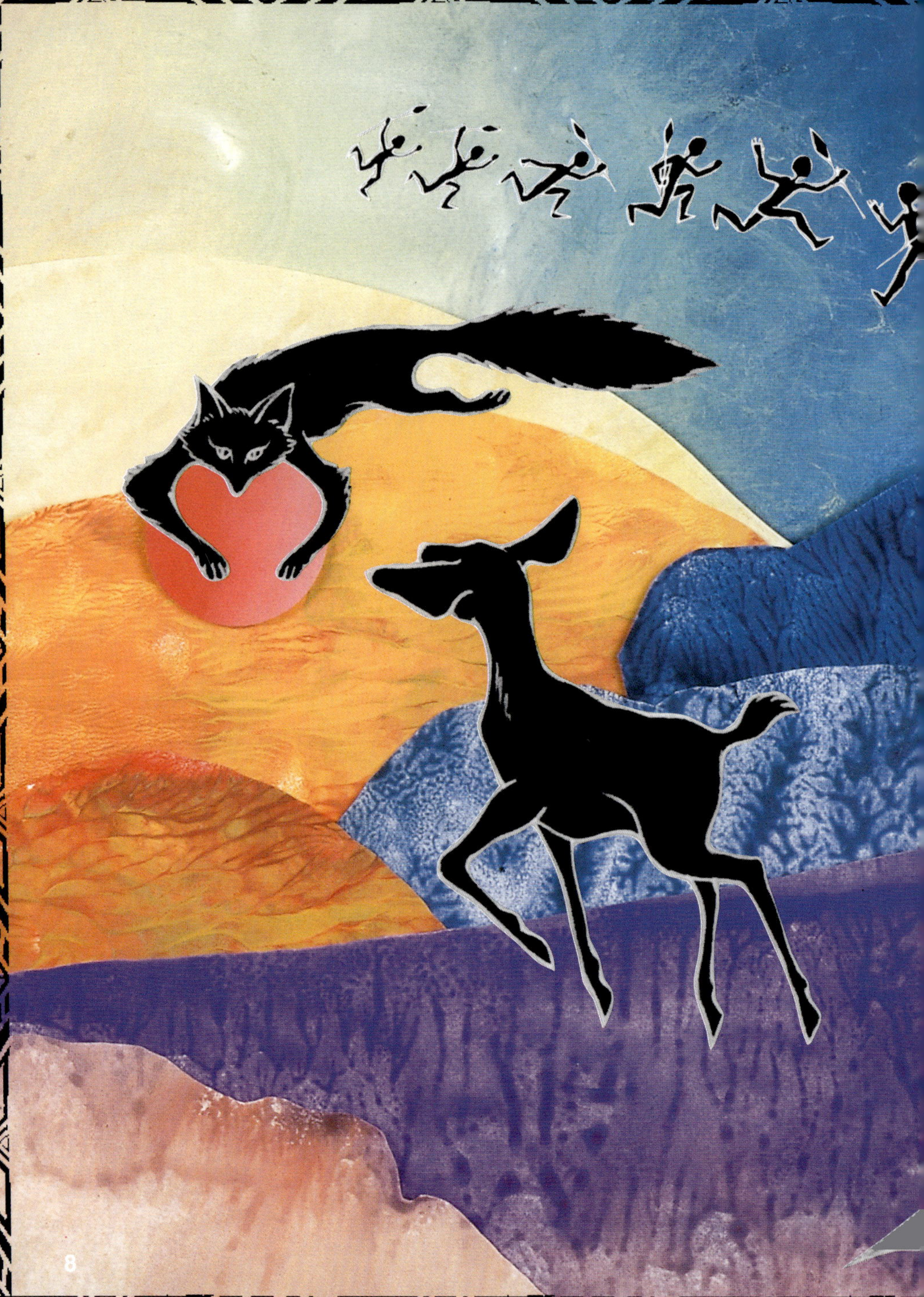

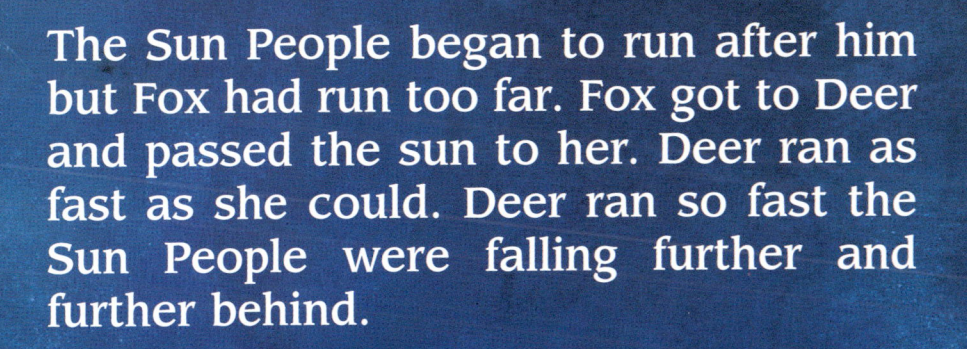

The Sun People began to run after him but Fox had run too far. Fox got to Deer and passed the sun to her. Deer ran as fast as she could. Deer ran so fast the Sun People were falling further and further behind.

Deer passed the sun to Magpie. Magpie ran as fast and as far as she could. Then she passed the sun to Saynday. The Sun People just couldn't catch up.

By now the Sun People were such a long way behind, Saynday didn't have to run. He took the sun to the dark side of the world and made it shine. Everyone on the dark side of the world was happy now that it had light.

But soon all the people said, "We have too much sun now. It's too hot and too bright."

So Saynday threw the sun high into the sky.

"Now it can be bright and dark on both sides of the world," he said.

Maui and the Sun

A New Zealand Legend

Maui was a hero of the
New Zealand Maori.

Long long ago in New Zealand, the days were very short. The sun would come up and race quickly across the sky. People found it hard to get their work done, and children didn't even have time to play.

One day, Maui said, "I'll catch the sun and slow it down."

The people laughed at Maui. Even his brothers laughed at him, but they said they would help him catch the sun.

Maui told his brothers to make a big net. He said they would trap the sun when it started to come up.

Maui's brothers said, "The sun is very hot. It will burn our net and ropes."

But Maui showed his brothers how to make ropes and a net from flax.

The next day Maui and his brothers set off to find where the sun lived. It took them many days to find the sun.

Maui said, "We'll hide until the sun goes to sleep. Then we'll put our net over the hole the sun sleeps in."

While the sun slept, Maui and his brothers made walls of clay to hide behind. Then they placed the net over the hole where the sun was sleeping. They put branches and leaves over the net so the sun wouldn't see it.

Each of the brothers held onto a rope and waited. Soon the sun began to rise.

As the sun rose Maui shouted, "Now! Pull the ropes now!"

The brothers pulled on the ropes as the sun tried to get away. Then Maui hit at the sun with his magic club.

21

The sun cried out, "What are you doing? Let me go!"

"We'll only let you go if you promise to go across the sky slowly," Maui said to the sun.

"Your magic club has taken away my strength so I can only go slowly now," said the sun sadly. So Maui told his brothers to let go of the ropes.

As the brothers let go of the ropes, the sun kept its promise. It rose and went slowly across the sky. The people were all happy. Now there was time for them to do their work and time for the children to play.